C000186339

je me touche

This paperback edition 1st published in 2017
by Paradiso editores S.A. de C.V. & Delere Press LLP

je me touche © Jeremy Fernando

*

First published in 2017 by

Paradiso editores S.A. de C.V.
Insurgentes Sur No. 1915 - 901
Col. Guadalupe Inn
C. P. 01020
México, D.F.
www.paradiso-editores.com

Delere Press LLP
Block 370G Alexandra Road
#09-09 Singapore 159960
www.delerepress.com
Delere Press LLP reg no. T11LL1061K

All Rights Reserved

ISBN: 978-607-97140-5-5

je me touche

Jeremy Fernando

PARADISO EDITORES
DELERE PRESS

for, Berit Jane Soli-Holt...

CONTENTS

DANCING WITH TRAINS:
OR, ON 'JOHN DUFFY'S BROTHER'

Where else can you find someone
who has turned doing absolutely
nothing into an art form ...

—Saffron on Bubbles, *Absolutely Fabulous*

Not just *nothing* in relation to achievement
— after all, all that happened to John
Duffy's brother was waking up and
becoming « possessed of the idea that he was
a train ».[1] chugging off to work, returning
at lunch time, and having a revelation that
reveals nothing — but, more importantly,
that even as one can trace these momentous
events, they happen to one who does not
bear a name: without which, can one even
say with any certainty whom it happens
to? After all, « there are thousands of
Duffys in the world: even at this moment
there is probably a new Duffy making his
appearance in some corner of it ».[2] Here,
we might take note that in a draft of the
tale, he had a first name — « Hugh » — but
that it was lost by the final version.[3] But,

[1] All references to the
short story are taken
from Flann O'Brien,
'John Duffy's Brother'
in *The Short Stories
of Flann O' Brien*,
edited by Neil Murphy
& Keith Hopper,
Champaign: Dalkey
Archive Press, 2013:
54-58.

[2] *Ibid*: 54.

even though we know that fact — even as we know there is a movement of named to unnamed — we should be careful not to make too much of it. For, that would be the problem of making meaning where there might be none. Though, even as we say that, we should bear in mind Flann O'Brien's quip that « modern writing, it is hoped, has passed the stage when simple events are stated in the void without any clue as to the psychological and hereditary forces working in the background to produce them ».[4] However, as we probe deeper, as the saying goes, all we find is: « Flann O'Brien is a discovery of William Saroyan's but further than that, at this moment, we know nothing except that he is not William Saroyan ».[5]

A knowing of the *not*, a knowing of *what is not*: a knowing of *no thing, nothing.*

In fact, all we can know is that one morning, « on the 9th of March, 1932 … he became possessed of the strange idea that he was a train ».[6] Which is not the same as he knew he was a train: or that he became a train. But that the idea came into him, took over him, was whispered into him: and in all this, it is not too difficult to hear echoes of the *daemon.* Keeping in mind that the point when craft becomes art is the moment where the *daemon* whispers into one's ear, when one is possessed of the strange idea that there is the possibility of art. Not forgetting that art, beauty, and truth are intertwined:

[3] Flann O'Brien. 'John Duffy's Brother' draft 1000 words (2 December, 1938) in *Special Collections Research Center.*

The other version of the tale that was of great influence to the thinking of this chapter is Flann O'Brien. 'John Duffy's Brother' in *Story: The Magazine of the Short Story.* Volume XIX (July-August 1941), No.90: 65-68.

And since we are attempting to speak of trains, of movements, of moving trains and thought, we should try not to forget that a draft often blows under, blows through, even when the best of attempts have been made to seal, to conceal, to contain. Perhaps then, even as we are reading, are attempting to read, a particular version of 'John Duffy's Brother', all the other versions — some of which we have never seen, might never see — continue to whistle through, leaving little tracks, trails, through our thoughts; perhaps even leaving us stranded at cross-roads.

[4] *The Short Stories of Flann O' Brien*: 56.

[5] Contributors' notes from *Story*: 3.

and more importantly, in ways that are, that quite possibly remain, beyond one; thus, when the *daemon* whispers in one's ear, one knows nothing except for the fact that there is a whisper — the sound of nothingness itself is quite possibly what opens one to the possibility of art. After all, even as he *was* « certain that he *was* a train ». « no explanation of this can be attempted ».[6] To compound matters, « strictly speaking, this story should not be written or told at all. To write it, or to tell it, is to spoil it ... and the fact that he kept his secret and sealed it up completely in his memory is the whole point of the story ».[8] At first glance, one may think it contradictory that the tale begins with a declaration that the event is a secret and then goes on to reveal it. However, since there is no explanation given at either the point of conception nor at the end of his possession, nothing is actually said about why or how John Duffy's brother becomes a train: all that we know is that he *was*.

An immaculate conception.

Not just in the sense of being perfect, spotless, undefiled by explanations, externalities, reason; but more importantly, one that maintains its mystery, its secret — even as it reveals, veils as it unveils.

Striptease.[9]

Formal perfection.

[6] *The Short Stories of Flann O' Brien*: 56.

[7] *Ibid*: 54.

[8] *Ibid*: 54.

[9] Never forgetting that even as (s)he takes off all her clothes, even as (s)he unveils herself — is there ever even gender when one is stripping, or is it pure performance of gender; pure sex — there is nothing that is being revealed. All that appears under her clothes is skin, another layer, one that perhaps covers up even more than the clothes above it.

This reading of striptease owes a debt of gratitude to Jean Baudrillard.

And when we say *was*, we should pay particular attention to the notion of the past, passings, and memory. For, not only was John Duffy's brother sure that he was a train, he was « certain that he was a particular train, the 9:20 into Dublin »[10] — a train that preceded him, that came before him, that he now was. This suggests that even as he was possessed by the idea that he was a train, the very train that he was is one from his memory, is one that is recalled by John Duffy's brother himself. A possession by memory: seized by his own recollections. And here, we should recall the fact that the very first scene is one of a remembering: one where « sometimes, recollecting that his clock was fast, John Duffy's brother would spend an idle moment with his father's spyglass, ranging the valley with an eagle eye ».[11] Where remembering that he was early, that he had more time — not necessarily knowing it, but recalling it — he spent time trainspotting.

[10] *The Short Stories of Flann O' Brien*: 56.

[11] *Ibid*: 54.

Sitting at the dock of the bay,
Watching the tides roll away
Sitting at the dock of the bay ...
Wastin' time ...

—Otis Redding & Steve Cropper

Wasting time whilst being stuck on time, stuck to time. After all, one must not forget that « he stood absolutely still for twenty minutes, knowing that a good train is equally punctual in departure as in arrival ».[12] And here, it is not too difficult to hear echoes of Immanuel Kant, who — as legend goes — was known for being such a metronome that one could adjust one's clock to the time he took his walks. Almost as if *time* itself became his call to duty — where there is a movement of time itself from a personal time (for his walks) to a universal notion (for all to set themselves by: the time on their clocks). Thus, a movement of time from a particular to a universal. Where time moves from a notion — an imaginary correspondence between the movement of the sun and the manner in which we spend our days, in other words a convention — to a duty of sorts, a categorical imperative. Where time itself is what dictates our actions, as opposed to acts being set to, linked with, specific times. However, one should not forget that the moment the dossier of habit is opened, it brings with it registers of repetition, addiction, and the possibility of the habit writing itself into one's *habitus*: where what was initially a practise — in which there is a separation of what one is doing from the one doing it — is now indivorceable from one's self.

Where it is not like how « small boys sometimes like to pretend that they are trains ».[13] but that John Duffy's brother *was* a train.

Perhaps. this is where the dossier of *secret* that was opened earlier becomes crucial. For. we should try not to forget that a secret lies not in its content. but in the knowledge that. in knowing that. what is spoken of is secret: being privy to the date of my birth is only significant if one also knew that it is the password I use. Thus. it is not the meaning. the signification. that is crucial. but its significance. Which is why « the really important part of the plot. the incident which gives the whole story its significance »[14] is one where sitting down to lunch John Duffy's brother « felt something important. something queer. momentous. and magical taking place inside his head ».[15] But of which nothing more is said. can be said. can be known. All he knew. all that we can know. is: at that point. he was « no longer a train. but a badly frightened man ».[16]

Nobody ever said that one would always like what the *daemon* whispers. And. even worse if it remains unknown to us. a secret: for. one must never forget that a true mystery makes us shudder.

mysterium tremendum.

In other words — and in terms of secrets. what else can one do but speak in the words of

another — all that we can know is what is not.
the *nothing*.

Which opens the question. *why does the tale foreground its moments of fictionality?*: « for obvious reasons. the name of this firm is fictitious ... [and] of course. both [old Mr Cranberry and Mr Hodge's] names are imaginary ».[17] For. if nothingness were its premise. ground — or *abgrund*. if you prefer — then surely it would all be fictive. One could posit that it is to maintain the secret. or at least certain secrets: which is ostensibly why « we will refrain from mentioning [John Duffy's brother] by his complete name ».[18] However. by setting aside certain things as « fictitious ». it also opens the possibility that others are not. Which is not to say that we should attempt to sift what is fictive from what is fact — that would be too banal. For. one should not forget that the significance of this event was that it was *magical*: the point at which fact and ficti on come together: fictive as it is beyond. outside of. reason. *ratio*. measurement. accountability. and yet fact insofar as it inscribes itself upon one's experience. body. self. And all John Duffy's brother can do is to testify to his experience: keeping in mind Jacques Derrida's lesson that fictionality is both the condition and the very limit of testimony: that without the *possibility* of fiction. there would not be the possibility of testifying to one's experience. In Derrida's words: « testimony

[17] *Ibid*: 56.

[18] *Ibid*: 54.

always goes hand in hand with at least the possibility of fiction, perjury, lie. Were this possibility to be eliminated, no testimony would be possible any longer; it could not have the meaning of testimony ».[19] He continues: « in order to remain testimony, it must therefore allow itself to be haunted. It must allow itself to be parasitized by precisely what it excludes from it inner depths, the possibility, at least, of literature ».[20] However, « the essence of testimony cannot necessarily be reduced to narration, that is, to descriptive, informative relations, to knowledge, or to narrative: it is first a present act». And here, since it has to be a « present act ».[21] we have to reopen — recall — the dossier of memory. For, in order to testify to an experience, one has to have first lived through it; thus, all testimony occurs through memory. However, since one has no control over, nor access to, forgetting — it happens to one — not only can one never be certain if one has forgotten anything in the testimony by way of omission, one can also never know if every act of memory entails, brings with it, forgetting. And, since there is no limit to the number of testimonies one can offer regarding a particular event, this suggests that not only is forgetting possibly in every testimony, it is only because of the possibility of forgetting that every, and any, testimony can occur.

Thus, it is the impossibility of knowing, the impossibility of certainty — forgetting itself

[19] Jacques Derrida. *Demeure: Fiction and Testimony*, translated by Elizabeth Rottenberg. Stanford: Meridian, 2000: 27.

[20] *Ibid*: 30.

[21] *Ibid*: 38.

— that allows for each and every testimony. Thus, not only is forgetting the very condition of testimony, it is another name for fiction itself.

Thus, foregrounding fictionality opens the register that fact itself — insofar as fact is what one can verify, what has referentiality, the correspondence between a notion and something in the world — is premised on fiction.

Thus, it is not just that « testimony cannot necessarily be reduced to narration », it is also — and at the very same time — conversely true: narration, fiction, literature, cannot be reduced to testimony, to a present act. For, even as John Duffy's brother might well be testifying to the fact that on the morning of the 9th of March, 1932, he was a train, the fact that he was a train cannot be divorced from the telling of himself as a train. And it is the telling itself that confronts us with the mystery, the secret — the significance even — of the tale.

Which is why there was no way to end the tale, if one can call it an ending, other than to echo Keat's 'On First Looking into Chapman's Homer'. And, in particular, the moment of silence, the inability to speak, as one is first faced with what is beautiful — never forgetting the warning of Kant regarding the dangers of the sublime: and Plato on how art, how what is beautiful, can ruin one. Both the beautiful and the sublime can quite literally move one beyond oneself. leave one « a badly frightened man ».[22] make one other than one self: make one a wreck. or even a train. And it can throw one completely out of whack. derail the train. so much so that « when he got back to the office [the man who's drink was stout] had some whiskey in his stomach and it was later in the afternoon than it should be ».[23] Where the sublime. the beautiful. can rupture time itself — perhaps turn it into. open one into experiencing it as. one's personal. singular. time — if only for a moment. And perhaps. the error — if one wants to conceive of it as a mistake — that John Duffy's brother makes is to open himself to the possibility of attending to the imaginary. to imagination. to responding to the possibility that he was a train.

Perhaps here. we should momentarily attend to the fact that he becomes a train the moment the notion. the « idea ». that he is a train enters him. Thus. the moment he is seized by the thought of being a train. he becomes a train: the moment the idea passes from him. he is no longer a train. This is far beyond the notion of correspondence between the word « train » and the idea of a train: this is no longer about referentiality. This is language as language: where language opens to the very possibility of itself as language. Where what is uttered *becomes. is.* Which is why the tale could

[22] *Ibid*: 58.

[23] *Ibid*: 58.

only open with the warning that « to write it or to tell it is to spoil it »[24]: not because it ruins the secret (that can never happen), but more importantly that it cannot be recounted: that all that is remembered is the fact that it is already forgotten. Where nothing can be known but:

John, I'm only dancing
She turns me on, but I'm only dancing
She turns me on, don't get me wrong
I'm only dancing

—David Bowie

Which is not to say that « only dancing » has no effects. Far from it. But, that even as it affects all those involved — the two dancers and John — the only thing that can be known is that there is dancing.

Movement ... of thought, of tales, perhaps even of trains.

Which suggests that: all there is, is in the telling.

Perhaps here, we — I am now taking you along with me — should take a little detour, a slight change in tack, track, and open our receptors to the lesson of Scipio from Cervantes' *The Dialogue of the Dogs*, who teaches us that « ... some stories are enough by themselves, and their wit lies in the story itself. With others, it's all in the telling.

11

I'm here to tell you, some can entertain without any throat-clearing or wordy frills. But others you have to dress up in words, to make something out of nothing with eye-rolling and gestures and whispers. That way, even a dull, thin, depressing story can become piquant and juicy ».[25] Bearing in mind O'Brien's quip that every thing in modern writing matters, the fact that it is a dog telling us this should not be lost on us. Not just in the sense that every thing, facet, of the tale contributes to it; not just the fact that the distinction between the foreground and background are blurred; but, more importantly, that the moment something is uttered, it is so. How it comes to be so occurs in the movement of the tale, its rhythms, cadences, schedules, timing, which can only come about in hearing it, reading it. Where the reader, the one who listens, attends, opens her very self, to it.

« To write it or to tell it is to spoil it »
— for, the tale occurs in its listening, reading.

Of course, it would be absurd to suggest that one can read, listen, if it is not written, spoken, told — but we should remember that we are in the realm of the *magical*: where reason is both present (or we would not be able to read, listen) and, at the same time, taking a walk, on its own track. Where both reason and unreason (if one can call it that) are not contradictions, but possibilities.[26]

[25] Miguel de Cervantes. *The Dialogue of the Dogs*, translated by David Kipen. New York: Melville House Publishing, 2008: 28-29.

[26] Which is not to say that I should — even if I could — tell you the significance of Scipio being a dog. For, as Berganza — his interlocutor — quips, « ever since I could chase a bone, I've longed to talk … » (25). Perhaps, all we can do, as Scipio says, is « whatever happens, let's talk. Omen or not, if something's meant to be, nothing on earth can stop it. There's no point arguing over how or why all this is possible … » (25).

And perhaps, it is precisely through foregrounding our inability to say why it — why something — is so, that we acknowledge its significance: the power of its telling; the magic of story-telling itself.

Where, it is precisely forgetting that allows it to be so.

For, if memory were certain, there could only be one possibility: either correct or otherwise. Where, all utterances would be constative. The fact that John Duffy's brother could become not just a train but a particular train that he had previously known of by being possessed of the idea, opens the possibility that this possibility is one that had been previously forgotten. Which means that utterances are no longer in the realm of truth-falsity, nor even of performativity, but that utterances *are* — they call into being possibilities that might well have been forgotten. But since they are forgotten possibilities, or since there is at least a possibility that they are forgotten, one can never be sure of what occurs, one can never be sure of the effects of one's utterances, until it happens. Until the moment it happens, one can only

like stout Cortez, when with eagle eyes
He stared at the Pacific — and all his men
Look'd at each other with a wild surmise—
Silent, upon a peak in Darien.

—John Keats

Perhaps here, we should return all the way to the beginning, both of the tale, and this attempt to read it. And attend to another possibility of « to write it or to tell it is to spoil it » : extending it to the point where any attempt to understand it, bring it under one's conception, is to ruin it. At this juncture, it is not too difficult to hear echoes of Jean Baudrillard's poetic reading of poetry: « the poem ... lacks nothing: any commentary makes it worse. Not only does it lack nothing, but it makes any discourse appear superfluous. Poetry and thought are to be taken in their literalness, not in their truth: truth merely makes things worse ».[27] Thus, all we can do is to attend to the tale in its telling. Much like how Mr Hodge and Mr Cranberry respond to John Duffy's brother's nod to « Herr Marx » — by taking him absolutely seriously (« that's communism! » ... « he means... that it is now first class only »), that is, to the very point of absurdity.[28]

To the point where Marx refers to the possibility of both Karl and Groucho.

Where all we can know is *what is not.*

Where possibilities remain, where what can be remains, in the forgotten.

In the *perhaps only to come.*

And here, as we are nearing the proverbial end, it might be tempting to attempt to tie it up nicely, too neatly, with an Agambenism:

[27] Jean Baudrillard. *The Intelligence of Evil or the Lucidity Pact,* translated by Chris Turner. London: Verso, 2005: 211.

[28] *The Short Stories of Flann O' Brien*: 57.

where possibilities, potentialities, are a *potential-to-be* and a *potential not-to-be*. However, this misses the point that if there is a *potential-not-to-be* it is no longer a potential: which is not to say that potentiality is merely a prelude to actuality — far from it. However, for potentiality to remain in potential, it must have a *potential not-to-be* that is still within potentiality itself: thus, it is always a *potential to-be* and an *impotential not-to-be*. Where there is a possibility of negating itself as a negation, but where this double negation is neither a positive (in the sense of a to-be) nor does it completely cancel itself: thus a negation that negates its negation, that *shimmers as a possibility*.[29] Where it is perhaps even — if we take it to its very end — a potentiality that has already happened, but which remains in potential: for, its becoming remains beyond us.

[29] This reading of Agamben's notion of potentiality was opened to me in a conversation with Werner Hamacher.

Thus, both an *only to come* and also a *has already come that remains to come, that remains beyond us.*

Where we might well be moved, transformed, by something we know not of.

Where we might well already be moved, transformed, even though we know not.

Where it might well be us that « to this day ... starts at the rumble of a train in

the Liffrey tunney and stands rooted to
the road when he comes suddenly on a
level crossing — silent ... »[30]

[30] *The Short Stories of Flann O' Brien*: 58.

Where. at some moment in time. we might
just be — or perhaps already are — a 9:20
train ...

YES, I WOULD PREFER NOT TO:
OR, FOR THE LOVE OF...

I tell you yes.
I begin us with a yes. Yes begins us.

— Hélène Cixous

And it is this « us » that is the site of thought. For, in order to begin thinking, we have to open a relationality between our selves and something, or someone, between our selves and another.

Where, thinking begins with a « yes ».

But in order for that relationality to be opened, one would first have to be open to that, to its, possibility. Thus, it is an openness that precedes thinking, even as much as one is thinking as one opens that relationality; it is — and we might never quite be able to say with any certainty what 'it' is — both the condition and an approach to the possibility of thinking itself.

And here, we have to attend to the fact that

it is not *one* who « begins us with a yes »
but an « I ». So, not only is it an active
decision, it is one that is made by a singular
person — and in that moment of deciding,
the « I » cannot escape, retreat, hide behind,
universality: there is no duty, imperative,
framework, that makes that decision for the
« I ». It is only such as *I have chosen* it
to be so. « I » have called « us » to begin
with that « yes ». In fact, the decision to
begin must have come before that « yes »
— even as it can only come as the « yes »
is uttered. Thus, opening to a relationality
with another resides in the « yes » : « yes »
being the very condition and juncture of the
relationality we are speaking of.

But if opened by an « I », then perhaps
it is only that of Hélène Cixous. And by
reading her « I », do I then also make it
mine, make her mine? Which opens the
question of its legitimacy: for, my reading
of her « I » may never have had anything
to do with her: the « I » might well be only
voices in my head. Which might suggest
that one has moved back into the realm of
an imperative, a duty, a call : but where one
can never quite be certain from where this
call is emanating, where it is coming from.
So, perhaps the risk here is not just that by
responding to a call one might make it one's
own, but that the very acknowledgement
of the possibility that it might be a call already
opens the possibility of « us » : an « us » that could
only happen because of the intervention of

the « I ». The answering that might have already happened when one says « yes » to the possibility of the call, to the possibility that it is a call.

An openness, an opening, that resides in a « yes » *even as yes, it, is only opened by an I.* A « yes » that is preceded by a *yes-ness* of the yes: *a yes-ness that can only be called into being by an I who cannot yet know of it.* Or, perhaps even a « yes » that always carries with it *a yes-ness that escapes the yes.*

For, even as the « yes » is opened, this is an affirmation that cannot be a complete affirmation: if that were so, this would be a « yes » that completely consumes the object that it is purporting to open a relationality with — at that point, the object or person that the « I » is in a relationality with is subsumed under the self: which would be the end of the possibility of that relationality.

In other words, even as there is a « yes », in order for it to be an opening to thinking, it has to always also carry the possibility of a *no* in it. And if thought is an openness to possibility — otherwise it would merely be a moment before action, be a precursor to doing — there then has to be the potential for thought to not only amount to nothing, but also be non-thought itself. However, this would not be a non-thought that is an antonym to thinking, but a thinking that thinks itself as non-thinking, or a non-thinking that is always already also thinking: a *no* within a « yes » : a no that quite possibly carries echoes of *yes-ness* within it: the two perhaps remaining indistinguishable.

*

I would prefer not to.

A response — Bartleby's response — foregrounding the fact that it is the « I » that « prefers not to » : not that 'I cannot' nor 'I will not' but that this is a preference. That it is not based on anything other than a decision by the « I » : for, when asked « *why* do you refuse » by Mr B. his boss. Bartleby's response is simply, « I would prefer not to ».[1] Thus, to read this response, Bartleby's response, as an absolute refusal would be untrue: just because he « prefers not to » does not mean that he will not.[2] But just because it is not a complete rejection of the request also does not mean that it is a delayed compliance: Mr B comes to realise, rather quickly, that « his decision was irreversible ».[3]

So, even as it an inclination — and like all preferences, one that might well be unjustifiable — its effects, in relation with every situation, every moment in which there is a response, are lasting.

Quite a few thinkers — Giorgio Agamben and Slavoj Žižek amongst them — have attempted to read Bartleby's response as a form of passive resistance: their claim is that his response, which is always also a non-response, short-circuits the system. If he had out-rightly rejected Mr B there would have been an immediate expulsion, an instant firing: « had there been the

[1] Herman Melville. *Bartleby the Scrivener: a story of Wall Street.* New Jersey: Melville Publishing House, 2008: 19.

[2] *Ibid*: 25.

[3] *Ibid*: 20.

least uneasiness. anger. impatience or impertinence in his manner: in other words. had there been anything ordinarily human about him. doubtless I should have violently dismissed him from the premises ».[4] The trouble was. as Mr B continues. « there was something about Bartleby that not only strangely disarmed me. but in a wonderful manner. touched and disconcerted me ».[5] And here. Mr B makes what one might call the fatal error: « I began to reason with him ».[6]

Whilst most readings. readers. focus on Bartleby. perhaps we should momentarily turn our attention to the other interlocutors. those who are attempting to elicit not just a response but a particular act. action. from him. I — allowing all echoes of the unjustifiability of my choice — would like to propose that they were unable to move him. influence his actions. have power over him if you prefer. as they structured their statements as requests. And. in doing so. not only did they open the possibility of non-compliance. it was a far more fundamental mistake: requests function on the logic that both parties involved are operating under the same rules. form. customs. reason — in other words. the exchange is one that involves pre-set options. and not actual choices. That in a situation. to echo Mr B. « a slight hint would suffice — in short. an assumption »[7]: the assumption being that the one receiving the address would know what. the right thing even. to do.

4 *Ibid*: 18.

5 *Ibid*: 19.

6 *Ibid*: 19.

7 *Ibid*: 45.

Perhaps, what is truly subversive about Bartleby's response is that it takes Mr B's questions seriously: takes it as a question which offers the potential for a true response. And in doing so, Bartleby challenges authority to reveal itself — to not hide behind the illusion that it is offering a choice. That even as Mr B thinks otherwise, authority is no more than « vulgar bullying ».[8] In other words, what Bartleby does is to challenge daddy to show himself.

[8] *Ibid*: 42.

Here, we should try not to forget the register that Avital Ronell opens in *Loser Sons*, where she teaches us that authority is hinged around the figure of the origin (*auctor*), the source, the father. And, it is important to note that authority rests in, revolves around, the figure — more than the person, the body — of the father. For, if daddy has to impose the whip, he no longer has any authority: it is only truly authority when one does not have to use any force. In other words, authority triumphs when one is doing what daddy expects: without him having to say, let alone do, anything.

Authority is based on no more than a hint, an assumption.

Thus, the one who is authoring authority is not so much daddy but the one under his authority — one writes, authors, authorises, one's own subjugation. And, we find Mr B coming to grasp with the true radicality of

Bartleby's response in his summation of his scrivener's replies: « you are decided then, not to comply with my request — a request made according to common usage and common sense ».[9] Bartleby's challenge lies in his refusal to accept a prescribed notion of « common » : his insistence that even though he is a scrivener, he can inscribe his version, or at least open a negotiation, of what is common in any particular situation. To compound matters, it was not as if Bartleby could be threatened, coaxed, or even bribed to alter his position:[10] which might be what is truly terrifying about his response. And here, it is not too difficult to hear echoes of why the Khmer Rouge were particularly frightening: it was not as if there were no other regimes that were fond of killing their own people: it was the fact that they were utterly and completely incorruptible, that they could not be persuaded there was another possibility, that they were so eager to follow their own rationale, their own rationality, that they were beyond reason itself.[11]

Perhaps one can also contend that Bartleby's insistence on his position — even to his own detriment: he ends up in jail, and eventually is assumed to have died alone and penniless, or at least to have drifted away forgotten by everyone except perhaps Mr B — demonstrates an inability to learn. Thus, Bartleby might well be, is quite possibly, the figure of the

[9] *Ibid*: 20.

[10] *Ibid*: 41-44.

[11] For a haunting account of the early days of Khmer Rouge Cambodia, please see François Bizot. *The Gate*, translated by Euan Cameron. London: The Harvill Press, 2003.

Much of the text hinges on Bizot's uneasy friendship with his captor Douch, developed over the three months he spent as the latter's prisoner. Far from being a brutal captor, Douch is portrayed as a principled idealist, completely incorruptible, and totally committed to the cause. But it is not as if the Douch that is better known — the Douch that is head of the infamous S-21 torture centre — cannot be detected as well. In that sense, it is not a descent into brutality, a fall of the man in spite of his ideals, the idea, but that the murderous rampage is part of the ideology itself. And no where is this better captured than in Douch's own words: « It's better to have a sparsely populated Cambodia than a country full of incompetents! » (119).

idiot *par excellence*. And it is the radical stupidity of the idiot — the refusal perhaps to see. learn. be infected by. the symbolic structure of language — that always keeps it (for gendering the idiot would already bring it. tame it. under language) *avant la lettre*. pre-language. *infans*. And thus. quite possibly always also open to the possibility of language itself.

And the figure of the *infans* invites us to opens the dossier — or in the spirit of things. the register I am foregrounding. that I would prefer to foreground. is — that Bartleby's response brings with it the possibility of *making his own choice*. An imaginative response: one that refuses the boundaries that the other assumes one would draw for oneself. That takes the possibility of language itself seriously. and by doing so echoes Nietzsche's reminder that each act of writing (*schreiben*) possibly brings with it a scream (*schreien*): one that tears open. rips apart. punctures. quite possibly undoes precisely what is written. ascribed. let alone prescribed.

The scream of the scrivener. as it were.

Where. the effect of Bartleby's response is not just on the possibility of his own imagination. but also on the imagination of his boss: he becomes an « intolerable incubus »[12] to Mr B. We see this most obviously in the incident where Mr B.

[12] *Ibid*: 50.

25

at his wits end. since Bartleby refuses to budge. decides to move. However. even after he has done so. Bartleby continues to be a spectre in his life — letters are sent to Mr B's new office requesting. almost demanding. that he does something about the one who « persists in haunting the building generally. sitting upon the banisters of the stairs by day. and sleeping in the entry by night ».[13] Almost a perfect manifestation of the Indignatos slogan in Spain: *si no nos dejáis soñar, no os dejaremos dormer.* (*if you do not let us dream. we will not let you sleep*). Where what has been occupied is not an office space — that would be too banal — but the very imagination of Mr B himself. Where he even begins to hear Bartleby in everything. even when people are not talking about his scrivener.[14]

Here. we can finally fully appreciate the futility in Mr B's lament: « since he will not quit me. I must quit him ».[15] For. even though there was an overt attempt to shift location. he always already knew that it would not work: he had long inscribed Bartleby into his being.

So. it is not just that in his statement « I would prefer not to » Bartleby is. as Agamben and Žižek suggest. being transgressive by becoming *anything you want me to be*; but. more radically. he has infected Mr B's imagination by being *in anything.* However. it is not so much that

[13] *Ibid*: 54.

[14] *Ibid*: 43.

[15] *Ibid*: 50.

Bartleby transfigures himself to fit in with the desires of Mr B. but that — by being such an enigma — he has seduced his boss into attempting to « reason with him » : and thus. input logic onto him. write onto him. Authoring Bartleby such that he becomes his *significant other*: keeping in mind that this is not of the order of meaning — it is not a relationship of signification. but significance. If one wanted to. at this juncture. one could channel the spectres of Gilles Deleuze and Félix Guattari and call it a relationality with a strong field of intensity. Whilst this might appear to be a throwaway comment — an opening of a dossier for no good reason — we should remember not only that we might be attempting to tread into a zone where reason has long left the building. but that it is precisely in these zones — these seeming moments of divergences. such as when he is walking along the street and overhears a conversation that has naught to do with his scrivener — that Mr B's thoughts go foremost to Bartleby. Here. we should recall the scene just before Mr B moves from his office. at the point when he is grappling with « resentment » towards Bartleby. where he is stopped by the recollection of the « divine injunction: 'A new commandment give I unto you: that ye love one another' ».[16] And. a love in the precise sense of opening himself to the possibility that is Bartleby: to the point of « construing his conduct. Poor fellow. poor

[16] *Ibid*: 47.

fellow! thought I. he don't mean anything: and besides. he has seen hard times. and ought to be indulged ».[17]

Where Mr B starts writing a Bartleby in order to justify his own acts. perhaps his own beliefs. even as much as we will never have access to that.

> Or perhaps. an attempt — in an attempt — to save reason itself.

> Authoring Bartleby — authorising Bartleby.

Thus. one could read *Bartleby the Scrivener: A Story of Wall Street* as a tale of resistance. a tale of how a singular response — in terms of each response happening in a particular moment. time. place. but also how the uniqueness of both Bartleby and his reply — ruptures the structure of authority. reverses it even as its irreversibility seduces the other to reverse itself precisely due to its irreversibility.

But that would be a slightly limited reading.

For. what would be left out is another possibility: that it is also a story of love.

For. one must never forget that authority requires relationality. that relationality is the very condition of authority: one must author the other before authority is enacted on oneself. Thus, always also a tale of opening oneself to the possibility of another, to being infected by another, to being inscribed by and inscribing another onto oneself: opened by Mr B's very first « yes » — from that moment henceforth, opening himself to Bartleby.

Not a « yes » that is of the order of reason — how was Mr B ever to know — nor a « yes » that is calculated.

But a « yes » that resounds with Hélène Cixous' reminder — her voice — that whispers ...

I love you: I work at understanding you to the point of not understanding you. and there. standing in a wind. I don't understand you. Not understanding in a way of holding myself in front and of letting come. Transverbal. transintellectual relationship. this loving the other in submission to the mystery. (It's accepting. not knowing. forefeeling. feeling with the heart.) I'm speaking in favour of non-recognition. not of mistaken cognition. I'm speaking of closeness. without any familiarity.[18]

[18] Hélène Cixous. 'What is it o'clock? or The Door (we never enter)', translated by Catherine A.F. MacGillivray in *Stigmata*. New York: Routledge, 2005: 106.

RAGING BULL, MEET RUNNING BEAR

A little over six years after the banners were raised, one is left with an overarching sense of futility. Almost as if the reawakening of the revolutionary zeal of the people, the masses, has had its moment in the sun — and now, it is back to business as usual. Both the Arab Spring and the Indignatos Movement in Spain, which inspired the Occupy Movement — and its accompanying protests, which initially spread like wildfire — seem to have amounted to nothing. After initial successes in Tunisia, it seems to have faded out: Egypt today looks no different from the days under Mubarak's regime; capitalism and New York are still identical twins; and despite a promising start in Hong Kong, it looks like it will remain the stock-exchange of China and not much more. One might even say that it is not as if this was anything new; many promising movements have faded away before: London had its Summer of Love in 1967; Paris had its May '68; perhaps every one just has a turn on the dance floor.

However, it is far too easy, too lazy even, to play world-weary cynic. For, this would ignore the fact that even though these events may not have played out in the manner one thought — even hoped — they would, their echoes continue to resound in us. Moreover, if one could know, predict, their exact outcomes, they would hardly be events. Thus, in order to potentially respond to the possibilities of the Occupy Movement, we should first attend to it in its singularity.

And perhaps, there is no better place to start than at the juncture of its supposed failure.

One of the first things to happen after the Occupy Wall Street protestors were evicted from Zuccotti Park, on 15 November 2011, was the caging of Arthur Di Modica's sculpture, the charging bull that has become synonymous with Wall Street. According to *The New York Post*: « Law-enforcement sources say the cops are keeping the barriers up to protect the sculpture from protesters who could vandalize the symbol of wealth and prosperity ».[1] This had, of course, been to the chagrin of tourists who now unable to snap pictures with the iconic symbol. To many, the bull captures the spirit of pure capitalism: a raging animal bearing down single-mindedly on a goal, at the expense of anything, and everything, in its path. Ironically, police protection of the bull did nothing other than cause the

[1] Rebecca Harshbarger & Frank Rosario, 'Outrage over Caged Wall Street bull' in *The New York Post*. (27 December, 2011).

further demise of local businesses in the area: « a sandwich server at Café Plaza on Broadway told *The Post* that the corral around the bull makes people think the area is closed off ». Perhaps the point they missed is that for capitalism to work, it has to be set loose.

But here, we should recall the fact that in December 1989, Di Modica had secretly dropped off the 7,000 pound bull in front the of New York Stock Exchange as a response to the recovery after the 1987 crash. Even then, the sculpture was seized by the police; and it was only massive public outcry and media attention that resulted in its eventual placement a few blocks away, outside Bowling Green Park. The fact that the bull was an artisan's response to a particular situation should not be lost on us: this echo certainly resonated with Micah White and Kalle Lasn of *Adbusters* who foregrounded the bull in their poster announcing the advent of Occupy Wall Street on September 17, 2011.[2]

[2] Amongst other places, a digital copy of the poster can be found here: http://upload.wikimedia.org/wikipedia/en/5/57/Wall-Street-1.jpg

And it is the notion of situation that is crucial here. Not just in the line from the said poster — « what is our one demand? » — but in the very spirit of the movement itself. After all, all *Adbusters* did was to put out the poster. « Occupy Wall Street, September 17, Bring tent » was, at best, a suggestion. According to White: « we basically floated the idea in mid-July into our [email list] and it was spontaneously taken up by all the people ... It just kind of snowballed from there ... They made it their own and ran with it ».[3] Thus, the movement was a result of people responding to a particular situation. And in many ways, it was precisely the spontaneous nature of the movement that made it difficult to police: the deterritorialised nature of the bodies ensured there was no head to cut off.

The police, though, seem to have taken their cue from riot-control specialist Rex Applegate: « if you are dealing with a crowd with no central command, the tactical approach is to segment it into units, creating 'clear zones', boundaries, and leaders. In fact, it is often necessary to organize a crowd by force in order to defeat it ».[4] In other words, it is not just that — to paraphrase Caligula — one wishes Rome had only one head so one could cut it off at one go, one has to go even further: one has to ignore the absence of such a head, imagine it into existence, and then cut it off. We see this most clearly in their

[3] Andrew Fleming, '*Adbusters* sparks Wall Street protest: Vancouver-based activists behind street actions in the U.S' in *The Vancouver Courier*. (September 27, 2011).

[4] As read in Finn Brunton, *Decontrol in Science, Music and War*. Masters Thesis. Saas Fee: The European Graduate School, 2005: 56. In this paragraph, Brunton is summarizing Colonel Applegate's riot-control strategies.

strategy of attributing the entire movement to White and Lasn: for, the first thing one has to do is name it into existence. If one wanted to be ironic, one could say that the crowd had read Deleuze & Guattari well: the trouble was that the police were even better readers.[5]

In this, one can hear an echo of the classic riddle of the two doors (one leads to freedom, and the other to death: one door always tells the truth, and the other only lies) in the strategy of the police. The usual take-away from the riddle is that by asking the right question — *if I asked the other door, which door leads to freedom?* — you will get the response you need. What is usually not attended to is the fact that you have to ask a question about the other door. It is only in this indirect manner, as it were, that one can get an insight to the conundrum. For, it is only based on the answer of the other that you can discern something about the status of the doors: it is pointless to attempt to discover which door tells the truth or which one lies. In fact, even after finding out which door leads to freedom, this fact remains veiled (and in terms of effects, completely irrelevant). Similarly, by attributing the events to White and Lasn, the authorities have bypassed the entire movement itself. And when pressed to respond to what is happening in the streets, the same gesture — in one manifestation or another — is utilised: *if they have so much*

[5] The notion of repressive state apparatuses relying on the same tropes as those fighting for greater freedom, movement, nomadology even, is hardly a new thing. The Israeli Defense Force has for quite some time been a proponent of what is broadly called contemporary philosophy. In Eyal Weizman's article 'The Art of War' (*frieze*, issue 99, May 2006) one finds the IDF commander, Brigadier-General Aviv Kokhavi, reconceiving the city as « smooth » rather than « striated » : rather than obey the conventions of the city, the IDF attack on the city of Nablus was « inverse geometry » — that is « the reorganization of the urban syntax by means of a series of micro-tactical actions » — in action. In Weizman's words, this « involves a conception of the city as not just the site but also the very medium of warfare — a flexible, almost liquid medium that is forever contingent and in flux ». Kokhavi further explicates: « this space that you look at, this room that you look at, is nothing but your interpretation of it. […] The question is how do you interpret the alley? […] We interpreted the alley

time to camp out and protest, why don't they just apply themselves and get a job.

A *non sequitur* even Silvio Berlusconi would be proud of.

In this sense, Slavoj Žižek's call for a concrete statement — « there is a long road ahead, and soon we will have to address the truly difficult questions — questions not about what we do not want, but about what we DO want » — or at least a concrete question — « maybe, the time has come to turn around these coordinates of what is possible and what is impossible: maybe, we cannot become immortal, but we can have more solidarity and healthcare? » — might well be moot.[6] For, it is yet another version of *if you ask the right question, you will get the answer you need.* The trouble with this is that at the end of the day — or to echo one of Žižek's favourite phrases, at the end of times — the answer still depends on the very system one is attempting to disrupt. Whilst one can argue that this is the very nature of communication — perhaps even politics itself — one needs to remember that they play the game of two doors rather well.

Maybe what is truly needed, as Simon Critchley puts it, is more of the impossible. For, Critchley contends that Žižek's emphasis on concrete questions is hinged on a commitment to violence — a rupturing, a breaking, in which he sees a version of

as a place forbidden to walk through and the door as a place forbidden to pass through, and the window as a place forbidden to look through, because a weapon awaits us in the alley, and a booby trap awaits us behind the doors. This is because the enemy interprets space in a traditional, classical manner, and I do not want to obey this interpretation and fall into his traps. [...] I want to surprise him! ». Shimon Naveh, Kokhavi's instructor, continues, and explains why the works of Deleuze & Guattari are crucial to the methods of the IDF: « several of the concepts in *A Thousand Plateaus* became instrumental for us [...] allowing us to explain contemporary situations in a way that we could not have otherwise. It problematized our own paradigms. [...] In Nablus the IDF understood urban fighting as a spatial problem. [...] Travelling through walls is a simple mechanical solution that connects theory and practice ».

In all of this one can detect the teachings — and warnings — of Gilles Deleuze and Felix

Leninism.[5] Žižek's response, in his review of Critchley's *Infinitely Demanding*, is to point out that making such 'impossible' demands is a manner of submission, surrender: for, « since they know that we know it, [that such demands cannot be met,] such an 'infinitely demanding' attitude presents no problem for those in power ». Hence, « the thing to do is, on the contrary, to bombard those in power with strategically well-selected, precise, finite demands, which can't be met with the same excuse ».[8]

Perhaps what both Critchley and Žižek miss is the fact that they are actually saying the same thing. In the latter's finite, precise, strategic demands, lies an echo of the infinite: for, when Critchley is speaking of the infinite, it is an attempt to open up possibilities within demands (after all, he certainly understands that *asking for the moon* is a metaphor). For, one should never forget that when Lenin asks « what is to be done? » the true radicality of his question is that it remains an eternal question: at each point, there might be a specific, particular, response to this, but even within the momentary answer (if one insists on that term), lies the same question.

The demand:

not for answers, nor certainty, but for nothing other than possibilities: for the right to demand.

Guattari themselves: the gesture of deterritorialisation is always met with an attempt to reterritorialise, to instrumentalise. Both the state and the subjects are playing on the same field; what remains crucial is *who is more imaginative*.

The IDF and their relation to the works of Deleuze and Guattari was first brought to my attention by Manuel de Landa during his seminar *Deleuze and Science* at the European Graduate School (June 2007); and this dossier was reopened by a timely reminder from Vincent van Gerven Oei during a recent email exchange (June 2012), and also during a conversation with May Ee Wong (November 2012).

[6] Amongst other places, a transcript of Žižek's speech at the Occupy Wall Street moment on 10 October, 2011 can be found at http://www.versobooks.com/blogs/736

[7] Simon Critchley. *Infinitely Demanding: Ethics of Commitment, Politics of Resistance*. London: Verso, 2007.

Running Bear loved Little White Dove
With a love big as the sky
Running Bear loved Little White Dove
With a love that couldn't die

— Jiles Perry Richardson

It is all too easy, too tempting even, to read the Occupy Movement as a call for a return to nature: a reversal from uncontrolled capitalism to an earlier — purer — time, when life was simpler; a return to the soil. Where Little White Dove on top of our raging bull would be saved by her hero, Running Bear. After all, the gap between the 1% and the 99% is as wide as the « raging river » that separated them: compared to this divide, the split between the Capulets and the Montagues seems nothing other than a neighbourly spat. However, the romanticisation of a past age — based on ideas and ideals that perhaps never existed — is not only problematic, but runs a further risk: one should never forget that most of the horrors throughout history were based on totalising ideas: notions that efface the particularity of situations. To compound matters, one only has to look at Khmer Rouge Cambodia to see that oftentimes the road to hell is paved with good intentions.

There is, though, much to learn from Running Bear: in particular, his act of jumping into the river in spite of the impossibility of swimming across, in full knowledge that he was plunging to his own death. This could well be the response of the protesters to the standard conservative reaction of *instead of standing around, why don't they get a job*: by rejecting the logic of the 1% (grabbing everything at the

[8] Zizek's review of *Infinitely Demanding* can be seen at Slavoj Žižek, 'Resistance is Surrender: What to do about Capitalism' in *London Review of Books* (15 November, 2007).

expense of everyone else), the protesters short-circuit capitalism itself. For, the logic of greed requires everyone's participation: by refusing to engage in the same logic, by giving the other what (s)he demands without a fight, the entire game itself collapses.

As Jean Baudrillard teaches us in *Symbolic Exchange and Death*, « the only effective reply to power is to give it back what it gives you, and this is only symbolically possible by means of death ».[9] And this is precisely why the suicide bomber is the figure that scares us the most: not the one that is dead (for, once that has occurred, the loses can be calculated, accounted for, rationalised, put back under reason), but the one that is to come. The suicide bomber who is ready to die, that has already chosen the side of death, is the one who haunts us: for, there is no defense available. Her death has already been counted: all we have to do is pay our end of the bargain, perhaps just not yet. This is « death [that] is neither resolution nor involution, but a reversal and a symbolic exchange ».[10]

Death as a challenge.

As their hands touched
and their lips met
The raging river pulled them down
Now they'll always be together
In their happy hunting ground

[9] Jean Baudrillard, *Symbolic Exchange and Death*, translated by Iain Hamilton Grant. London: Sage Publications, 2007: 43.

[10] *Ibid*: 156.

And this opens yet another question:
what's love got to do with it?

Traditionally, literature regards death as
the supreme demonstration of love: in order
to prove one's love for another, one must
die, or at the very least be willing to give
up one's life. But this would, of course, be
completely missing the point. For, the death
in love is not a physical death, but rather
a death to other people, other possibilities.

In other words —
a symbolic death.

Which can be found in the moment of the
« I do ». For, in this utterance lies a nod
to madness: the decision to spend the rest
of one's life with another has no *grund*,
is not based on anything other than a
futurial, imagined, possibility. In other
words, the moment one says, « I do », one
is reifying time itself. Which also suggests
that at the point of the « I do », the two
who exchange this vow — keeping in mind
that promises have no referentiality, and
thus, no possibility of verification — are
opening, are opening themselves to, the
possibility of an eternal: where the future
and the present collapse into one. For,
this is the only way in which *when two
become one* is possible: it could never have
been about people, but about time itself:
a promise that is made about the future.

which is always in the past (when said, it is already over), lived out in the present. And here, it is not too difficult to hear echoes of Søren Kierkegaard's notion of love: « the eternal in erotic love is that in its moment individuals first come into existence for each other ».[11] Where the coming together is precisely the opening of the relationality between the two: a relationality that opens the possibility without any possibility of knowing what this possibility is.

Where, the « I do » is nothing other than an affirmation of possibility.

Where, in responding to the call of the poster from *Adbusters* — keeping in mind that the movement organically developed, and thus, no one knew exactly what they were showing up to, or for — each person that turned up was saying their very own « I do ». Perhaps here, we might even posit that by responding in the affirmative to a question, what was being affirmed was nothing but the question itself. Hence, all criticism that there is no concrete question that is asked is moot. By opening the possibility of the question, the potentiality of questioning, the people on the streets have opened — channeling Critchley and Žižek — an infinite question within a finite question.

Détournement at its finest.
The imagination of the police was to cast

[11] Søren Kierkegaard. *The Seducer's Diary*, translated by Howard V. Hong. Princeton: Princeton University Press, 1997: 111.

a *corpus* — a head with a body — to the movement, and then enact their eviction on the very same body that they created. The imaginative response of the body is to play at questioning the system: as if there were a central authority that can answer their demands, as if there were any demands in the first place.

And what is foregrounded is nothing other than the fact that Wall Street itself is a name for nothing.

We find this to be particularly true in Singapore's version of the movement, where Singaporeans were called to Occupy Raffles Place on 15 October 2011 via a Facebook group posting. Predictably, the authorities reacted by deeming it unlawful. In a statement responding to media queries, the police said they had received reports that a netizen is « instigating the public to stage a protest gathering ... in support of a similar protest in New York ». It continued: « Police urge members of the public not to be misled and participate in an unlawful activity ».[12] The fact that only a handful of people — mostly foreigners and journalists — turned up is usually regarded as a sign of its failure; or even worse, a sign of the apathy of Singaporeans. The more skeptical Singaporeans dismissed the entire thing as a joke. But one should never forget that there are few things more unsettling than the uncomfortable silence that follows a

[12] Tessa Wong. 'Police warn against unlawful Occupy Raffles Place protest' in *Straits Times Online* (14 October, 2011). Raffles Place is Singapore's equivalent of New York's Wall Street.

failed joke. The non-protest demonstrated, in a way that no actual protest could have done, the very nature of the state. The irony that only the police showed up for a protest was not lost on anyone: the sight of them enforcing nothing only served to remind everyone that capitalism itself is based on nothing: as long as there is productivity, maximum performativity and, most importantly, surplus value, it can be *anything you want it to be.*

The very opposite scenario was seen on 26 November 2012 in Singapore, when 171 bus drivers working for the Singapore Mass Rapid Transit (SMRT) — aggrieved at unfair working conditions — refused to show up for work. After a reprimanding from the state — through its various ministries — for « an illegal strike » (workers in « essential services » such as public transportation have to give 14 days notice before a strike) which damaged the « industrial harmony » some of the drivers returned to work — leaving only 88 to continue the next day. By the third day, « 20 SMRT bus drivers were brought to the police headquarters for investigations » : and on the 29th, four of the alleged ringleaders were charged in court. One of the drivers « faces an additional charge of making an online post about the strike ... calling his fellow drivers to *take action* ». But, it is not as if the bus drivers were not saying exactly the same thing as the absent protesters

at Occupy Raffles Place. However, their
error was not just in exposing the running
logic of Singapore (that people are a
resource expected to be dancing to the
same tune), nor even in highlighting the
fact that workers are exploited differently,
but in saying the unsayable: that this very
« industrial harmony » is hinged upon
its very opposite — in order to sustain
this « harmony » what is needed is the
disharmony of workers themselves. This is
exemplified in the fact that no other bus
drivers — let alone workers in any other
sector — joined the original 171 in the strike
(even though it was a justifiable grievance
— that they were paid less than other
drivers doing the same thing — the same
complaint that just about every worker has).
And here, the imaginative nature of the
state was demonstrated: by foregrounding
the notion that it sympathised with the
drivers — « 'we understand the grievances
of SMRT drivers and it's unfortunate that
they sought to resolve this matter through
organising an illegal strike.' said Minister
of State for Transport Josephine Teo » —
but that, according to Minister of State for
Manpower Amy Khor, « what has happened
has damaged this industrial harmony that
we have built up over the years and swift
action must be carried out », there was a
shift from the content of the strike to its
means. The performance of reluctance by
the state — *we only stepped in, as it was*

illegal — transfers the focus from the very target of the protest (that disharmony of workers — *the last thing that we want is for workers of the world to unite* — is the perverse core of harmonious industry) to the protesters themselves (if everyone else is fine with being disharmonious why do you have to try and call for everyone to stand together). In this manner, the state has turned the very thing that the protesters have foregrounded (disharmony in harmony) back on themselves — a true demonstration of *détournement*.[13]

Thus, the true error of the 171 bus drivers was an error of form: the error of attempting to confront the proverbial beast. For, that only serves to strengthen the illusion that there is something to confront.

Instead of the error of facing it head-on, of declaring that capitalism is an empty signifier, one has to jump into the very illusion. This is the lesson of Wes Craven's *A Nightmare on Elm Street*: the only way to defeat Freddy Krueger is to take him on his own terms. For, it is pointless debating whether he were real or not (the effects of Krueger in one's dream were real enough): in fact, speaking about him is the most dangerous thing one could do (once one knew about Krueger, one was open to a potential night call). One had to just accept the notion of Freddy Krueger, jump into

[13] Sharon See. 'Four SMRT bus drivers charged with instigating illegal strike' in *ChannelNewsAsia*. (29 November, 2012).

As of 3 December, 2012, « 29 ex-SMRT bus drivers who received stern warnings and had their work permits revoked for their role in last week's illegal strike — over pay and living conditions — were put on flights back to China yesterday afternoon, the Home Affairs Ministry said … 150 others who participated in the illicit sit-in, however, would be warned — as they had shown remorse or were coerced into participating — but allowed to remain and work here provided they continue abiding by Singapore's laws ».

Teo Xuanwei, '29 "active participants" in illegal bus strike repatriated' in *TODAYonline*. (3 December, 2012).

The first driver to be charged, « for his involvement in the illegal strike last week was sentenced to six weeks imprisonment this afternoon, after he pleaded guilty to commencing an illegal strike ».

the dream and kill him there: the logic that threatens is potentially the very — one might even say, only — thing that saves.

For, dreams are quite literally worth fighting for. And if they don't let us dream, we won't let them sleep.

Hussain Syed Amir, 'SMRT bus driver sentenced to six weeks jail for starting illegal strike' in *TODAYonline*. (3 December, 2012).

*

Perhaps here, we might go back to the beginning, to the charging bull, keeping in mind that it was an artisan's response to a situation. And whenever one thinks of artisans, of the possibility of art, one can also hear echoes of Plato's warning — that art is potentially dangerous and can lead one away from being a good person.

When Arthur Di Modica dropped off his sculpture in front of the New York Stock Exchange in December 1989, he was responding to and with — in the precise sense of *reading* — the situation. And as Paul de Man never lets us forget: « not that the act of reading is innocent, far from it. It is the starting point of all evil ».[14] And, *evil* in the precise sense of asking a question: a question that opens, that might never be answered, that remains a question. For, we must never forget the potential heresy in all questions, the echo of the primordial question that resounds in all questions, the question we read in *Genesis* 3:1 — « did God *really* say, you were not eat to eat from any tree in the garden?' ... »

[14] Paul de Man. *Allegories of Reading: Figural Language in Rousseau, Nietzsche, Rilke, and Proust.* New Haven: Yale University Press, 1979: 194.

Perhaps now, the time has come for us to read Di Modica's sculpture. Keeping in mind the lesson from *12 Monkeys* and the *OBEY* posters: the appearance of a symbol on the walls captures the imagination of the people.[15] And, just because the sculpture has been there for the last 28 years does not mean that it cannot be new: not only is the

[15] A collection of the *OBEY* poster series can be found here: http://www.obeygiant.com/archives

situation different, the context new, each time one reads, one attempts to respond to, connect with, connect to, another. And here, it might be helpful to turn to Avital Ronell and, in particular, her meditation that « the connection to the other is a reading — not an interpretation, assimilation, or even a hermeneutic understanding, but a reading ».[16] Reading as an opening, an attending to: reading that responds with whilst opening possibilities.

Reading as imagination.

And now — perhaps more than ever before — we should keep in mind Paul Virilio's slogan from May '68: *all power to the imagination.*

But, this does not mean there are no risks involved.

For, if reading is an opening to possibilities, its effects — and the manner in which they affect one — are unknown until they occur. Moreover, if each reading is a response to, it always already involves a choice, a choosing, of one over another. And since one cannot fully know what one is selecting until it is selected, this is a selection without *grund* — an act of violence: picking one over all others, quite possibility without any legitimacy. Thus, each time one reads, one cannot be sure not only if one has mis-read,

[16] Avital Ronell. *The Telephone Book: Technology, Schizophrenia, Electric Speech.* Lincoln: University of Nebraska Press, 1989: 380.

over-read, or under-read, one cannot be certain if one has even read.[17]

Therefore, reading as possibility itself is *power to the imagination* in the precise sense of: one has to imagine that one is even able to respond to the situation and then to do so as if one can.

If the state can walk through walls, why can't you?

For, a true disruption comes through reading the notion that we are dealing with — responding imaginatively, with an artistic gesture. Perhaps, what the SMRT bus drivers could have done was to strike without having a strike. By taking the logic of « industrial harmony » itself to its limits — by driving in such accordance, in one tune, to the schedule of the industry, the bus schedule — what might have been foregrounded is not only that public transport is no longer about serving the public but about transporting, moving, herding, resources — the public as resource — in the service of a harmonious industry.

En bref, human resource management.

For, if power were truly in the hands of the people, surely they should be able to choose whomever they want — a true choice instead of picking from alternatives. And what is a more democratic vote than

[17] I explore the notion of reading as a pre-relational relationality which attempts to respond to nothing but the possibility of reading more fully in *Reading Blindly: Literature, Otherness, and the Possibility of an Ethical Reading.* New York: Cambria Press, 2009.

putting the name of whomever one wants in power, regardless of — in spite of — the persons presented on the voting slip. In this manner, regardless of who wins, the symbol chosen by the people will always haunt the incumbent.

Not only would the candidate that won through the system be discredited, not only would the democratic system be called into question, the people would have actually spoken.

The people would have actually dreamed.

ticktockticktocktick
tockticktockticktock
ticktockticktocktick
tockticktockticktock
ticktockticktocktick
tockticktockticktock
ticktockticktocktick
tockticktockticktock
tickcrosstickcrosstick
crosstickcrosstickcross
tickcrosstickcrosstick
crosstickcrosstickcross
tickcrosstickcrosstick
crosstickcrosstickcross

[18] This was first published as 'Dream Sleep' (with photography by Alice Renez Tay) in *Berfrois: Intellectual Jousting in the Republic of Letters*. (2 October, 2014).

écrit.cri.écrit
cri. écrit. cri.[18]

By diving into that river.

For perhaps, what we need is to take the message that we have been bombarded with — that *nothing is impossible* — seriously. And, read it alongside the other message we are not allowed to forget: that the good times are over, that we need to tighten our belts, and most importantly, that *the state owes us nothing*.

And *demand* what we have been owed: *the impossible*.

*

A version of this piece was first published in *Berfrois: Intellectual Jousting in the Republic of Letters* (December 2012).

AFTERWORD:

This practice, extraordinarily rich
and inventive, in particular as
concerns masturbation, is prolonged
or accompanied by a production of
forms, a veritable aesthetic activity,
each stage of rapture inscribing
a resonant vision, a composition,
something beautiful. Beauty will no
longer be forbidden.

— Hélène Cixous

... where writing and touching are no longer separate. separable. Keeping in mind that Cixous is attempting to open the possibilities of writing. open writing as possibilities. tease out the possibility that writing maintains a tearing. opening. scratching. each time it inscribes. That even as it is the marks of the inscriptions that allow us to begin to see writing — even as marks. inscriptions. are the beginnings. are quite possibly the start. of all reading. as it were — what has been scratched out of the parchment. paper. stone. medium. continues to haunt what is scratched into.

Or. in her own words: where « writing is the very possibility of change ».[1] Bearing in mind that writing changes the very surface. thing. site. onto which it is written. Where change is both what is written. and what allows writing to happen.

[1] Hélène Cixous. 'Laugh of the Medusa' translated by Keith Cohen & Paula Cohen in *Signs* Vol. 1. No. 4 (Summer 1976): 879.

Where change is writing itself.

Where the gaze of the gorgon. where looking upon her. turns one not into stone. into the permanent. the unchanging. but unleashes the possibility of laughter. rupturings. openings — dare I say. joy: not just pleasure. but perhaps even bliss.

Never forgetting that even as I am trying to cite her. quote her. bring her into conversation with us. I run the risk of performing — no. I inevitably perform — a

violence on her work. on her. Perhaps even
enact a terror on her — as much as I would
like avoid it. deny it even. For. each time
one calls out to her voice. as if in a *séance*.
or more precisely. marshals her voice for
one's own lines. one sentences her to a role
in the scene one is setting: for. one is always
also already speaking for her. through her.
summoning her as if she were one's.

prosopopoeia

as if she were I.

But. assuming — and admittedly this
requires a leap of faith — that one is
calling out. reviving. animating. her voice
because one agrees with her. because she
says something in a way that one can only
dream of doing so. because one — I — hear
in her text something that I would like to
say. would have liked to have said. suggests
that in that moment. she and I are no longer
quite so distinct. so distinguishable. That
at that moment. I am saying what she says.
what she had said. as if I had said it. as if
I am saying it. as if she had said it for me.

And at that very moment. she might well
be I. as I might be her.

And that. since only one voice — my voice —
is foregrounded in this speech. in speaking.
in this inscription. as I write. as I utter. I am
always also keeping her in the background.

But, it would be unfair, or at least I would like to think that it is, to say that all citations, all quotations, are mere appropriations. After all, there is much care that is put into them, both in terms of what is cited, and how it is done. One might even say that one is curating the voices one is bringing forth as one is building the piece that one is writing. Thus, even as one might be creating as one writes, even as one might be cremating the one whom one invokes in writing, as one is writing, perhaps even in order to write, one is always also preserving at the same time. For, to care is also to lament for (*charon*), quite possibly to grieve, to feel sorrow for (*karon*), or even to cry, call out, scream (*gairm*). A scream (*cri*) that quite possibility comes with, echoes in — even if one is never quite able to hear it — every act of, moment of, writing (*écriture*).

Perhaps then — assuming one is attempting to maintain that balance, tension, between caring for, bringing forth, *life*, and curing, preserving, *death* — one might well have to utter a scream whilst writing. But perhaps, not so much a cry of anger, but that of joy, amusement, of wild abandonment, of living, all whilst recognising the absurdity that one is always also solidifying, molding, making static, sculpting into stone.

Or, perhaps even — the one who cares is the one who laughs whilst inevitably carving into stone, *qui rire le rire de la méduse*. For, one has no choice but to form. to give a form to. even as one might try as much as one can to keep open. to maintain possibilities. But. even as one is shaping. one is constantly reminded that each scribble brings with it a little scratch — and perhaps even a little rip. a puncture. a *punctum*. Forgetting as it is memorialising: where every memory brings with it the possibility of forgetting: where forgetting is both the condition of. and limit to. memory.

Where the moment of writing. the moment of utterance. is the point when memory and forgetting come together.[2]

Touch each other.

Keeping in mind that one has no control over. no ability to know. forgetting. And thus. can only glimpse it as a part of memory that remains unknowable. A part that one *feels* is there without any possibility of knowing so. Which suggests that the point at which one *feels* is the point where one knows one is feeling but at the same time never knows. perhaps forgets. why one is feeling: the point where all that one knows is that one is feeling: where all that one is feeling is feeling itself.

Where perhaps. all that one feels is oneself feeling.

Where. all that one feels is oneself.

[2] Keeping in mind Jacques Derrida's reminder that an archive « shelters itself from [its] memory which it also shelters: which comes down to saying also that it forgets ».

Jacques Derrida. *Archive Fever: A Freudian Impression*, translated by Eric Prenowitz. Chicago and London: The University of Chicago Press, 1995: 2.

So, even as it is a collection of memories — ostensibly for the purpose of sharing, making public — it is a place that is guarded, not just by the *arkhon* (lord, ruler), but by the fact that it is always put together, enframed — thus, incurring choices, selections, pickings, as well as exclusions. In other words, once archived, it is both open and closed at the same time: one is invited, free even, to see, but the invitation to view is guided, under an *arkhé*, and there are rules. And once the register of framing is opened, one must also never forget that to frame something, someone, is to accuse another of something they haven't done, or at least, might not have done: to make them guilty. Which is not to say that archives

And at the risk of completing a trinity of voices, here it might be apt to open our registers to Jean-Luc Nancy's reminder that « a subject *feels* (*se sentir*): that is his characteristic and his definition [and also her, always also her, definition: at least in my remix of Jean-Luc]. This means that [s]he hears (himself), sees (himself), touches (himself), tastes (himself), and so on, and that [s]he thinks himself or represents himself, approaches himself and strays from himself, and thus always feels himself feeling a 'self' that escapes (*s'échappe*) or hides (*se retranche*) as long as it resounds elsewhere as it does in itself, in a world and in the other ».[3]

are false, at least not necessarily so: but it is precisely in the attempt to frame the truth — to ground a certain version as true — that lies its crime.

And if conceiving, a conception of, the self is the starting point of all thought — for, even if one posits that relationality is the opening gesture of thinking, it is first and foremost a subject, no matter how unstable, how multiple, that attempts to think, or recognise, this relationality — this suggests that before the possibility of thinking, or at least at the moment when thought is opened, there is first and foremost *feeling*.

[3] Jean-Luc Nancy. *Listening*, translated by Charlotte Mandell. New York: Fordham University Press, 2007: 9.

A touch.

A touch between: for, one should also bear in mind that a touch is a relation. And more precisely, a touch between two notions, opened by a subject who feels the possibility of thinking these notions — and at the very moment of recognising the possibility of touch, of a relation, at the very moment the subject feels that *I might attempt to think this relationality*, perhaps before even this cognitive moment of thought, perhaps in the moment when the *I opens the possibility that it is the I who thinks*, the self is feeling nothing other than itself.

Where at the opening moment of the possibility of thought, all that happens is *I touch myself*.

Thinking ... feeling ... speaking ... sighing ... writing ... writhing ...

*

Thinking is an affair of the ear.
— François Noudelmann

Or, perhaps: thinking is an affair with
the ear; thinking is my affair of the year.
Not quite just a relationship between
thought and the ear,[4] between thinking and
hearing, but perhaps a secret relationality,
a surreptitious relationship, one in the
dark, one that remains veiled from all,
perhaps even from the one in that relation.

Where thinking involves being in tune with
the object that one is in thought with, but
perhaps in ways that remain unknown to one.

Which opens the question: *can one, can
we, ever be in tune?* Or, *is one only ever
in tune with?* Always already a relation, in
relation — where being in tune is not just
being with another, but premised on there
being an other.

Thus, a touching.

Where being in tune is a touch. Fingers,
words, sounds. So, even as touching
another involves language — in the form
of something to be shared by the ones
involved — one might consider tuning in to
Roland Barthes' reminder where, echoing
Lucretius, he offers the possibility that
« language is a skin: I rub my language
against the other. It is as if I had words
instead of fingers, or fingers at the tip of

[4] François
Noudelmann, *The
Philosopher's Touch:
Sartre, Nietzsche,
and Barthes at the
Piano,* translated by
Brian Reilly. New York:
Columbia University
Press, 2012: 75.

my words ».[5] Though, even as the two are in touch, are touching, another voice — that of Nancy — never lets us forget that « it is space that one first needs to touch ».[6]

So, even as there are two or more in relation — in a relationality — what one is in tune with is a *space between.*

And quite possibly what one is attempting to listen to, as one is tuning one's receptors to the possibility of another, is that space, to *what is not.* Where being attuned with — where the tune — lies in the *not-.* Where the dash is precisely the space needed: never forgetting that even as it connects, it can also break, be broken.

Dashed.

Even as this dash can only be seen but not heard.

An unheard, perhaps unhearable, sound that potentially detunes one's self as one attempts to tune into another.

And here, one should bear in mind, recall the dossier earlier opened, that citation is also an attempt to resound, to be in tune, with the voice of another. A homage, a touching, that always also potentially wounds. That not only echoes another, but perhaps always also steals, takes over, away, or at least alters, her voice. An attuning, attunement, that always already detunes

[5] Roland Barthes, *A Lover's Discourse: Fragments*, translated by Richard Howard. London: Vintage, 2002: 73.

[6] A thought, a notion, that Jean-Luc touched me with during a seminar at the European Graduate School entitled *Art, Community, & Freedom*, in June 2006.

both the self, one, and the other that one is attempting to be in tune with.

Thus, a relationality that potentially undoes all tuning.

A *détunenement*, if you will.

And yet, at the same time, both, all, in the relationality, are always also already in tune with each other. However, since they are quite possibly detuned, this suggests that this is a tune that lies outside the boundaries of knowability. And if potentially beyond cognition, this also suggests that it is a tune that comes from elsewhere. Thus, a tune — an attunement — that is, that can only be, *felt* by those in the relationality.

A tune that tunes them: but perhaps moves them in manners that remain unknown to them.

Auto-tune.

Thus, a tune that tunes itself, whilst potentially detuning those in the relationality. A tune that might be felt by those in relation, but where not just how they are attuned, but what the tune is, might remain beyond them. Where the tune is not just unknown, but perhaps not even heard — just felt. But, just because it is not heard does not mean that one cannot say whether it is good or bad, whether one likes it or not. Much like art — as Henry Miller claims in his letter to Anaïs Nin. For. according to Miller. « art is not the translation or the representation or the expression of some hidden thing. It is a thing in itself — pure. absolute. without reference. In whatever medium you choose to employ. the mastery of the medium constitutes the art. There are no rules. no guideposts. But one can detect bad art from good art — or better. one can detect art ».[7] Thus. if one attunes oneself to the medium of one's work. one can detect a certain something called art. that one calls art. that perhaps only one calls art. Where. there might possibly be a certain quality to the something that moves it beyond the medium. beyond craft. *tekhnē.* but perhaps only through. and with. its medium.

[7] Letter from Henry Miller to Anaïs Nin, 10 April, 1933 in Gunter Stuhlmann (Ed.) *A Literate Passion: Letters of Anaïs Nin & Henry Miller 1932-1953.* New York: Harcourt Brace & Company, 1987: 143.

[And if I'm continuing to call it. *it.* it might well be due to the fact that I have no idea what else to call it — or. what its proper name should be. is.][8]

[8] An admission that perhaps can only be admitted to, be admissible, in a parenthesis: a little frame so as to allow me the possibility of uttering, *I was framed.*

And perhaps. if it is a certain quality that we are attempting to think of — even if the object of that thinking might be escaping us. be slightly beyond us — it might well be this quality that we are attempting to tune ourselves to. be attuned to.

A certain *timbre* of thought. as it were. And here. it might be the point to open our registers once again. retune ourselves. to Jean-Luc's thinking. in particular. to the point when he says, « I would say that timbre is communication of the incommunicable: provided it is understood that the incommunicable is nothing other, in a perfectly logical way, than communication itself, that thing by which a subject makes an echo — of self, of the other, it's all one — it's all one in the plural ».[9] For, as Nancy continues, « communication is not transmission, but a sharing that becomes subject: sharing as subject of all 'subjects'. An unfolding, a dance, a resonance. Sound in general is first of all communication in this sense. At first it communicates nothing — except itself. At its weakest and least articulated degree, one would call it a noise. (There is noise in the attack and extinction of a sound, and there is noise in sound itself.) But all noise also contains timbre. In a body that opens up and closes at the same time, that arranges itself and exposes itself with others, the noise of its sharing (with itself, with others) resounds: perhaps the cry in which the child is born, perhaps an even older resonance in the belly and from the belly of a mother ».[10]

An original sound —

perhaps an echo from, of even, an origin. Not that one can have access to this moment: or, even if one did, not that one would, could, know of it. For, even as one speaks, attempts to speak, of origins, of an *auctor*, one should try not to forget that one

[9] Jean-Luc Nancy. *Listening*: 41.

[10] *Ibid*: 41.

is always already quite possibly authoring. altering. it.

Perhaps here. one should slow down. rewind slightly. and pay attention. tune our antennae. to the fact that as Jean-Luc speaks about timbre. as he attempts to communicate his thoughts on communication and the incommunicable. he opens with an « I would say » (*je dirais*). One could say — I could say here — that it is him taking responsibility for his claim on timbre. for his thought. him hiding behind nothing. no one else. But. it is a touch more than that: for. *je dis* would have already foregrounded the singular position. A « would say ». opens the possibility of an utterance that is not quite yet. an utterance that is to come. almost as if he is speaking for the Jean-Luc that says. that would have said. that could only know. what timbre might be at some point in the future. And at the point when Nancy utters « *je dirais* » this is a Jean-Luc that only can *feel* that this is what timbre is: the utterance is one where the « I » attempts to touch. attempts to respond with. timbre. in the very moment of speaking about. writing on. it. Where communication is the sharing. is the feel. is the touch. is the subject who remains a plural whilst always also singular.

Where in that gap between the singular and the plural. the very gap that is needed to touch in the first place. lies precisely the incommunicable: in the slight hesitation of the future possibility, of the *diraient*. Which does not mean that the Jean-Luc that utters does not know what he is speaking of: far from it. But that even in his certainty, even in the communicability of his thought, even in the potential communion *between his thought and the us, between him and the we* who tune our ears to him, in the timbre that is relationality itself, lies a certain uncertainty, a certain incommunicability — of the subject, of the one who feels, of feeling itself.

And perhaps here, it might be apt timing to adjust ourselves to another tune that was always also humming in the background, to the frequency of Lucretius, and in particular, his reminder that communication, that coming together, all communion, happens, takes place, in the *simulacra*, in the skin between.

Communication ... or, the trembling of the skin.[11]

*

[11] *Timbre*: 'characteristic quality of a musical sound'; from timbre 'quality of a sound'; earlier 'sound of a bell', 'bell without a clapper'; quite possibly earlier a 'small drum', probably through *timbanon* and *tympanon*, 'kettledrum'.

Still. timbre is not *a single* datum. Its very
characteristic is itself to be. more than a component.
a composition whose complexity continues to
increase as acoustic analysis is refined and as it
goes beyond mere determination of a sound by
its harmonics. Timbre is above all the unity of a
diversity that its unity does not reabsorb.

— Jean-Luc Nancy

A coming together: where the two in the relationality remain wholly other, remain irreducibly singular. Or, as Alain Badiou conceives, the moment of love: keeping in mind that the coming together that is called love is a « construction, a life that is being made, no longer from the perspective of the One but from the perspective of Two ».[12] For, one should never forget that the beginning of thought, the opening of oneself to the possibility of thinking, the opening of a relationality between oneself and an object, oneself and another, always also entails a possibility, a risk, that one's thinking, one's thought, one's life is *no longer from the perspective of the One but from the perspective of Two*. That one might well fall in love with the object of one's thought, perhaps even *fall in love* with thinking itself — and perhaps in ways that remain unknown, unknowable, to one, that one is veiled from, that one remains blind to.

And since the two in that relationality always remain other from each other, this suggests that the only possible glimpse, the only possibility of an insight, into the love another feels for one, is at the moment the other reaches out to touch one, attempts to communicate with one, utters to one, *I love you*. Where, as Roland Barthes beautifully tells us, « everything is in the speaking of it: it is a 'formula', but this formula corresponds to no ritual: the situations in which I say *I-love-you* cannot be classified:

[12] Alain Badiou with Nicholas Truong. *In Praise of Love*, translated by Peter Bush. London: Serpent's Tail, 2012: 29.

I-love-you is irrepressible and unforeseeable ... too articulated to be no more than an impulse, too phatic to be a sentence ... It is neither quite what is uttered (no message is congealed, sorted, mummified within it, ready for dissection) nor quite the uttering itself (the subject does not allow himself to be intimidated by the play of interlocutory sites). We might call it a *proffering*, which has no scientific place: *I-love-you* belongs neither in the realm of linguistics nor in that of semiology. Its occasion (the point of departure for speaking it) would be, rather, Music. In the manner of what happens in singing, in the proffering of *I-love-you*, desire is neither repressed (as in what is uttered) nor recognised (where we did not expect it: as in the uttering itself) but simply: released, as an orgasm. Orgasm is not spoken, but it speaks and it says: *I-love-you* ».[13]

[13] Roland Barthes, *A Lover's Discourse: Fragments*, translated by Richard Howard. London: Vintage, 2002: 149.

A burst. A musical burst. A burst as music. Or, music as burst — music to the point of bursting — music at the point of bursting. Or, perhaps even: music as the bursting point. Which also suggests that the point of love — at least insofar as one can hear its whispers — is also the point where Music bursts, is perhaps the point where it is no longer musical, is the point where it is quite possibly beyond the realm, the tone, of musicality.

Much like laughter. **éclat**

Where perhaps all one can catch — if we

can still speak of apprehending. *prehension*. comprehension — is a *feel* of music. A feel that one thinks is music. that perhaps at best one calls music. That might well be indistinguishable from sound. from noise. from a groan. cry. scream. or a sigh. That perhaps one imagines is possible to call. name even — keeping in mind that to name something is to prepare for its absence. its death — as music.

And here. at the risk of responding to a call from another voice. a voice of another — never forgetting that this call might well be only voices in my head — perhaps then. only feeling this call. one might be able to hear an echo of Anne Dufourmantelle's wish. perhaps even her plea. to « imagine that our culture would have not been led by language. that the senses — touching. hearing. tasting. seeing — would be the treasured paths towards wisdom: imagine that words would be only signs to secure our relation within a reality that would not need to be possessed. but simply visited ».[14]

[14] Anne Dufourmantelle. 'Desire and Sovereignty'. Open Lecture at the European Graduate School (16 August, 2013).

And perhaps. one might take her imagination just a little further — and dream of the possibility that language itself is sensual. is the skin between us that opens the possibility of touching. hearing. tasting. sensing. Clearly not language that is linguistic nor semantic. but language as a proffering — an offering of nothing but of the gap. the space between. And whilst the possibility of meaning, of cognition, of knowledge, is never effaced, language is always also the possibility of a gasp, a burst, a rupture — perhaps even a moment of rapture.

And if this is perhaps only a pipe dream, perhaps then I shall end here by offering up my own dream. That all I have said, have written, that my writing would be — to echo François Noudelmann's beautiful description of Roland Barthes' work — « a loving approach that is wary of being fitted into — bogged down by — some thesis ... »[15]

[15] François Noudelmann. *The Philosopher's Touch*: 99.

And if dreams are always already something that is beyond us, perhaps the only thing that one can say, I can say, that is left for me to say — allowing the irony that I can only say this by borrowing the voice of another, the voice of Jean Genet, to resound — is: « nothing I tell you will enlighten you. I await the poetical expression of what I have to say ... »[16]

[16] Jean Genet. *Miracle of the Rose*, translated by Anthony Blond. New York: Grove Press, 1966: 209.

Perhaps then, a pipe dream that quite possibly always also utters.

ceci n'est pas une pipe...